to my daughter Sharon,

giant slayer and servant of God.

I love you.

Contents

1 Sam 17:46-47

This day will Yahweh deliver thee into mine hand; and I will smite thee, and take thine head from thee; and I will give the carcases of the host of the Philistines this day unto the fowls of the air, and to the wild beasts of the earth; that all the earth may know that there is a God in Israel.

And all this assembly shall know that Yahweh saveth not with sword and spear: for the battle is the Yahweh's, and he will give you into our hands.

INTRODUCTION
FIRELIGHT BIBLE STUDIES

Have a seat and we'll dig into this wonderful story. My hope is that these studies are like sitting with your pastor next to a warm fire on a cold winter night. Others have gone to bed, but we're up, warm coffee at hand, while sensing one another's hunger for God's word. The conversation is sweet, at times deep, and at other times laughter is abundant.

There are few stories as famous as David and Goliath. The biblical story, found in 1 Samuel 17, has been the source material for movies, cartoons, sermons, motivational books, and Bible studies. Magic Mountain, a California theme park, has a roller coaster named Goliath because of its massive first drop. David and Goliath have also both been made into action figures. Of course, you should keep them together, because if you lose your David action figure you'll have to send Luke Skywalker after Goliath, and he might not be up to the task.

The themes of the story are well known, but the details

are easily overlooked. Why did David cut off Goliath's head? Why does 2 Samuel 21:19 say that a man named Elhanan killed Goliath? What happened to Goliath's sword? Why did Jesse send cheese with young David? Most important, what is this story really about?

So, grab your Bible and put a couple logs on the fire—it's time to have fun.

CHAPTER 1
BATTLEFRONT

I f you grew up in church, one of the first stories you learned as a child was the story of David and Goliath. What John 3:16 is to the New Testament, the story of David and Goliath is to the Old Testament. You may remember this children's song:

Only a boy named David, only a little sling,
Only a boy named David, but he could pray and sing

Only a boy named David, only a trickling brook,
Only a boy named David, but five little stones he took

And one little stone went in the sling, and the sling went round and round
And one little stone went in the sling, and the sling went around and around
And one little stone went in the air, and the giant came tumbling down!

We are so familiar with the story that we are likely to gloss over it when we read the Bible, thinking we know all the details. Let me ask you to back up and re-read the story of David and Goliath. Read it slowly, underlining and marking it as you go. Imagine yourself as David as the story is narrated.

The Battle Lines

At seventeen, David really is just a kid. Of course, seventeen-year-olds don't feel like they're children, do they? David's father, Jesse, called his son in from the field and asked him to deliver a care package to his brothers. The old man knew the boy was special because not long before, the great prophet Samuel had shown up in their hometown of Bethlehem and reviewed Jesse's sons. Upon seeing young David, Samuel had anointed the boy to be the future king of Israel. It was undoubtedly an event the older sons resented.

I wonder if Jesse told David privately, "Be careful not to speak about this. Remember how our forefather Joseph stirred his brothers' envy when he discussed God's plans for him with them? Don't let too many people know what God has chosen you for, or there could be trouble."

Back then, families were responsible for sending food to the frontlines to support the war effort and their family members. Jesse sent David with some corn and ten loaves of bread for his brothers. Jesse then gave David a second package to deliver: ten cheeses to the commander of their unit. This is like sending Hickory Farms to the battlefront. David was instructed to deliver the gifts and then bring Jesse back some news from the frontlines. Oh, I think David would come back with some pretty incredible news!

Why did Jesse give David cheese to bring to a battlefield commander? Because he knew it was important to be on good terms with the man who oversaw the welfare of his sons on the battlefront.

When David arrived, the army was gathering for battle, as it did every day. The Philistines are on one hill, looking down into the valley, and Hebrews on another. There are daily skirmishes between the two armies, but ultimately the battle has become a quagmire. Neither side is able to get the upper hand. Then the Philistines bring out their nuclear bomb—a giant named Goliath.

For forty days, the giant has been coming out to challenge Israel to end the standoff. He proposes the battle be reduced to a fight between two men. After all, war is so bloody and this one has been dragging on for a while now. Goliath is called a "champion" in the NIV. The Hebrew translation actually says he is a "man between the two"— that is, he is a warrior who is experienced in standing between two armies and settling the dispute by in a fight to the death with a representative from the opponent's army. The Israelites ran and hid when Goliath came out shouting.

When David heard Goliath's taunt and his curse against Israel and Israel's God, he asked what would be done for the man who killed the warrior. The reward turned out to be like winning a national lottery. Saul had already thought about what he would be willing to pay in order to get rid of this giant problem. The winner would receive monetary compensation. If that was not enough, the king also offered to give his daughter in marriage to the victor, making the man a member of the royal household. This is interesting, since Saul's daughter later falls in love with David, but Saul makes him jump through some pretty serious hoops before letting the young man marry his daughter. Finally, the icing on the cake for the winner would be tax-free status for his entire family.

That one's not bad—not bad at all! Imagine sitting back at Christmas time as gifts are given out. "Don't you have any gifts for the family?" someone questions.

"Ah, yeah, that," you say, leaning back a bit. "I have one gift for everyone to share."

Really? This has the markings of trouble, right?

"How about no more taxes. At all. Ever."

Yeah, you'd be pretty popular, all right.

David's brother Eliab overheard the boy asking about the reward, and he was ticked! He demanded to know why David had really come to the battlefront, and what had he done with his sheep. In fact, he taunted David a bit, noting that he cared for only a "few" sheep. We might understand his annoyance. He, and everyone else, just went running from a giant. Now his little brother is out there talking smack. Eliab must have thought the little guy was nothing more than a boy in a man's world. Frankly, David was making the family look bad.

David didn't drop the matter. In verse 30, he turns to someone else and asks them the same questions. David was interested in making sure the reward was an established thing that many people knew about. Ultimately David is motivated by faith in God and love for his nation. But I also think he may have seen this as a means by which God would bring blessings to his family.

David and Saul

What's Saul been doing for forty days? He's had time to publicize his reward, but there have been no takers. When he hears that someone has volunteered to fight the giant, he has them brought to him. What a surprise when he learns the volunteer is nothing more than a young boy.

David boldly told Saul that there was no reason for anyone to despair because he would personally go and fight the Philistine. This did not exactly ease Saul's concern!

"You are not able to fight him!" Saul said. Imagine, young David stands before the very king of Israel and is immediately chastised and dismissed as nothing more than an idealistic youth. Saul even explains the reasons David can't go: "Look, you're a boy, and he's a grown man. And this is no ordinary man; this man has been fighting since he was a boy."

David probably did not roll his eyes at this, but I wonder if deep down he grunted, "How is a boy supposed to become a warrior unless someone lets him fight?"

Patiently, David explained to the king of Israel that he was not just a boy who had been playing on the farm. He was an experienced shepherd who kept watch over his father's sheep. That might not sound dangerous, but sometimes a lion or even a bear would come and steal a lamb from the flock. David didn't just count that sheep a loss, but he would courageously go after the lost lamb and rescue it. In fact, David told the king that he had killed lions with his bare hands, grabbing them by the mane and slaying them.

David wraps up his speech to Saul with a sudden twist. If he could kill a lion or a bear—both fearsome creatures—then he should have no problem taking on the Philistine. But David doesn't just call him a Philistine; he calls him an *uncircumcised* Philistine. This giant isn't just a problem; he is a direct enemy of God. Goliath is outside of the covenant and thus vulnerable in ways Saul never considered.

> *David called Goliath an Uncircumcised Philistine*

David makes the entire situation a spiritual lesson. This is funny, because the boy is rather boldly schooling the king of Israel in matters of faith. If Eliab could have heard this, he would have blown a fuse—and they hadn't even invented fuses to be blown!

"You see," David explained to the king, "it was God who delivered me when I went to fight the lion and the bear. It wasn't me at all; it was the Lord who saved me. I can't beat a lion! But God can. This Philistine has challenged God himself, and God's going to make him like that lion and bear that I killed back in the fields of

Bethlehem. He has defied the armies of the living God."

Notice the line, "the living God." David believes that God is not an idol or a figment of his imagination. To him, God is a living being that he can have a personal relationship with. The same God who did great things for Moses, Joshua, Samson, and Gideon would give him victory.

Saul seems pretty beat down at this point. He can't send the boy away, or the kid might go telling the entire army that the king of Israel doesn't have faith in God. So what's a king to do? Saul tells David, "Go, and Yahweh be with you."

Armed for Battle

Before the boy leaves, Saul wants to make sure he has the needed tools. You certainly don't want to go giant hunting without your armor! Of course, David has come to the battlefield unprepared for warfare. He's just wearing an ordinary shepherd's tunic. Saul offers him his own armor and puts a brass helmet on David. 1 Samuel 9:2 tells us that Saul was a head taller than most people. Can you imagine a skinny seventeen-year-old trying to put on that man of war's armor? Not only was there armor and a helmet, but there was a coat of mail he put on the kid.

I love the movie *A Christmas Story*. Remember that scene when the mom bundles up Ralphie's little brother, Randy, to go out in the snow? She has him in so many layers of clothes his arms can't go down to his side and the poor kid can hardly walk. I picture poor David like that kid as Saul had his armor put on the boy. With a sword in hand, David tried to walk around, but it was just too much. The young man could hardly stand up.

"I can't go out like this," David exclaims.

He's simply not used to fighting that way. When he went against a bear or a lion, he simply used the weapons of a shepherd. So, as in previous entanglements, the shepherd boy went down to the brook and chose five smooth stones. Why five? Some have suggested that he meant to kill Goliath's brothers as well. I think his reasoning is more practical than that. There are many Philistines, and he doesn't know what will happen when the giant is knocked dead. It would be foolish to kill a giant and not have rocks ready to take on the Philistine army.

David and Goliath

David comes out for war with nothing more than his shepherd's gear. He's got a slingshot and a few stones and a shepherd's bag, but no sword or spear or grenade.

On the other hand, Goliath is huge. The NIV Bible reports that he is nine feet tall. That's two feet taller than Shaquille O'Neil. The Guinness Book of World Records

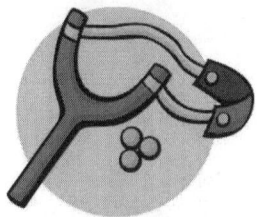

has cited American Robert Wadlow as the tallest man in history, coming in at 8 feet and 11.1 inches. This is a big guy!

I'm not sure that height alone is what the Bible focuses on when describing what a foreboding enemy Goliath is. He is trained and experienced in the representative warfare. Not only has he done this before, he lived to tell about it. His armor is 126 pounds. Add to that his javelin, which would have been a curved sword, and his shield bearer. He needs a shield bearer because he has so much stuff! The armor bearer is like his personal golf caddy. Goliath can choose the weapon of his choice to knock this kid down and get a hole in one.

The Philistine warrior is amused at what the Hebrew king has sent out to him. Is this a joke? A boy? 1 Samuel 17:42 says that when the Philistine saw David, he despised him.

"Am I a dog that you have come out to swat with sticks?" Goliath asked, amused and angered at the same time.

The Philistine cursed David. Have you ever been cursed? I have. It's not fun. It left me emotionally, spiritually, and even physically drained. Sticks and stones can break bones, but words hurt much more. God promised Abraham, "I will bless those who bless you, and whoever curses you I will curse" (Gen. 12:3, NIV). Goliath has now cursed David and he has cursed God.

"Come here, sonny," Goliath challenged. "When I'm done with you, the birds will feed on your corpse laying in this field. I'll turn you into dog food."

David wasn't going to back down now. "You've got a sword and a spear and a shield, but that's nothing." This is the moment we expect David to pull out his secret weapon. Does he have a bazooka? Because now would be a good time. "I come against you in the name of Yahweh of Hosts, the God of the armies of Israel whom you have cursed."

Of course, Goliath isn't scared by any of this. He's probably amused. He'll teach that boy a lesson in a minute. So he allows David to continue. The more the boy talks, the more stupid he's going to look when he's dead.

"Today Yahweh will give me victory over you. I'll kill you, and I'll cut your head off. And I'll feed you and the army you serve to the birds and the animals of the earth. They'll feed on your rotten corpses."

The "cut off your head" talk is interesting since David did not come to the battlefield with a sword. He's armed with a slingshot. His intent is not to wound Goliath; he plans to kill him. He knew all along that he would have to take possession of Goliath's sword. After all, he doesn't have an armor bearer nearby to help him switch clubs.

1 Sam 17:46-47 gives us David's concluding words to the giant. David says, "And the whole world will know that there is a God in Israel. All those gathered here will know that it is not by sword or spear that the LORD saves; for the battle is the LORD's, and he will give all of you into our hands" (NIV).

David's secret weapon is the name of Yahweh. This is not a magical name he is calling upon, but he is begging the living God to come down and rescue him. David is clear as day, isn't he? God doesn't save with swords or spears or tanks or nukes. God saves by his own mighty hand.

Fed up with the boy talking, the giant begins to advance toward him. Maybe he's concerned that after spewing all this faith the boy might run away and make Goliath look like a fool. He certainly doesn't want the kid to escape.

As Goliath begins his approach, David loads his slingshot and does something incredibly courageous—he runs toward the enemy. I'll bet the giant didn't expect that! In a hard, sudden motion, David slung the stone toward Goliath.

Did time stand still?

I wonder if in Heaven we are allowed to watch blu-rays of the great moments in history. If we are, I'll bet the one on David and Goliath is pretty well worn! How many people have come right to that moment when David shot that rock from the slingshot and then put it in slow motion?

David said in Psalm 144:1 that it was Yahweh who trained his hands for war. God had prepared David on a most unusual battle front: keeping sheep. In the daily work of shepherding, David had learned the skills needed to take on a giant. Not only had he learned to trust the Lord, but God had also developed his skills with the slingshot and prepared him emotionally for brutal conflict.

Ps 144:1

Blessed be the LORD my strength,
which teacheth my hands to war,
and my fingers to fight

David had told Saul that when he needed to, he had grabbed a lion by the mane. That's a big deal. Would you grab a lion by the mane? Probably not. But God was simply preparing David for more battles ahead.

The kid's aim was right on. The stone struck Goliath's forehead and knocked him down. Notice that the giant fell forward, striking the earth with his face.

The rock didn't kill Goliath; it knocked him down. I like this, because it means he had a moment to realize he'd been bested. David ran to the giant and picked up his sword. I'll bet it was heavy. David humiliates the giant by killing him with his own sword. Killing him wasn't enough; he wanted that big boy's head. I don't want to be too gross here, but cutting off a head would not be an easy task. David seems to have accomplished the work of decapitating the giant quickly.

The roles reversed and it was now the Philistines who were filled with fear and went running. I love it! Israel pursued the enemy, leaving their bodies strewn along the countryside for wild animals to devour. In fact, they chased them all the way home.

When the Israelites came home, David was brought before Saul, who seems confused as to exactly who this boy is. Saul's general, Abner, says that he also does not know. This has caused many liberal critics to suggest that the story is untrue, since David had earlier played in the courts of King Saul. Shouldn't the king remember the young musician? Not necessarily. Kings have many people come and go. When Saul got upset with the music and wanted to kill David, he threw a spear at him, indicating there was some distance between him and David. David was not there to have a conversation with the king; he was window dressing at that time. Saul had been interested in David's music, not his conversation.

Abner ran out, got David, and brought him back to King Saul. I like the mention that David still has possession of Goliath's head. Nasty, gross! But hey, when you're seventeen and you kill a giant, you have every right to want to hold on to his head.

A friend once said to me, "You know, David killed Goliath and cut off his head." Pause. I shrugged—so? "So, that just shows that David knew how to get '*a head*' in life." Great.

Saul appears to have only one question for David— what family did he belong to? This would both identify David for him and was necessary information if the king wanted to make good on his promise to exempt the family from taxes. David tells the king that he is David, the son of Jesse from Bethlehem.

David and Goliath, by Osmar Schindler (c. 1888)

CHAPTER 2
WHAT DAVID AND GOLIATH IS REALLY ABOUT

We get this story wrong.

Or, at least we miss the main point. Often this account is reduced to a "what's your Goliath" scenario.

When my daughter Annie was afraid of bullies, I said, "Tell me the story of David and Goliath."

"He fung his fing shot and cut off his head," she said. I guess that pretty well sums it up.

The primary thrust of this account isn't really about defeating your personal giant, or even taking down bullies. I think the Bible includes this account to express to us the importance of God's kingdom. For forty days, Satan (in the form of Goliath) comes forth and challenges the kingdom of God. Look at Goliath's words in 1 Samuel 17:8-11; even he can't believe that the Hebrews aren't going to defend the nation.

"Am I not a Philistine?" the giant asks. Now that's pretty obvious. The next question is more to the point: is not the opposing army servants of Saul? Shouting in rage,

Goliath says he defies the ranks of Israel. He hates them. And he pleads with them to bring out a man so that he can crush him.

What is Saul, the king of Israel's response to this challenge? The Bible says he and the other Israelites are "dismayed," "terrified," and in verse 24 they all ran from him in "fear."

David arrives on day forty just in time to hear the Philistine warrior give his daily appeal for someone to come and fight him. He watches as the Hebrew soldiers run in fear. This is not what he expected to find. Why are the people of God running away?

"Wait a minute!" David seems to say to Saul and all of Israel. "Who is this unbeliever to challenge the kingdom of God? We should stand up to him. God's nation is at stake here; we don't have time to run around scared. We're children of Abraham. Moses was our leader. Come on, guys! If God could take down all of Pharaoh's army and humiliate the entire nation of Egypt, why are we afraid of this one Philistine? Do you really think God took us this far only to let us get struck down by one 9-foot ugly dude? I don't think so. Now it's our generation's turn to stand for the kingdom and make war on Satan."

Of course, David is quickly dismissed as young, idealistic, and annoying.

Saul and the Israelites undervalue the treasure of God's kingdom. Saul was not personally willing to fight for the kingdom—and he's the king! Saul was brave enough to chase David all over the countryside when his own reputation was at stake, but he didn't have the same courage to stand against Goliath. I don't think Saul lacks courage; he lacks commitment to God's work.

Life is About. . .

I was stunned at what I saw at former South African leader Nelson Mandela's funeral. I can't remember what anyone said because one thing overshadowed the entire ceremony. Do you remember it? The sign language interpreter stole the show. Standing behind the president of the United States, the interpreter was making some pretty strange gestures. What kind of sign language was that? Turns out I wasn't the only one wondering what in the world was going on with that guy. Upon investigation, the media discovered that he was not doing any sign language at all—he was just making up motions. He said he'd been off his medication for schizophrenia.

The world is doing very much the same thing when it comes to the purpose of life. Our culture is not telling us what life is really all about; they're just making up their own message. "Obey your thirst," says a soft drink company. "Look out for number one," is a popular slogan. Of course, number one is never God. Society will tell us that life is about money, promotions, sex, and personal freedoms.

None of that is true. The world is just making up its own messages.

What is life really about? Serving God and living for Him.

The Apostle Paul told the Philippians that he would rather die and *Life is about serving God* be with Jesus, but that God kept him alive so that he could continue to serve the Lord. We are here to serve God's kingdom.

David volunteered to go and fight Goliath because he believed two things: First, David believed that the kingdom of God and God's people were worth fighting for. Everything is not worth fighting for. In fact, a sign of maturity is knowing what to make a fuss over and what to let slide. Second, David believed that if he was fighting for a godly cause, he would have a God's blessing and empowerment.

God's kingdom today is His church. How valuable is the church? Jesus didn't give the church a quick hug; he loved the church to the core of his being. Jesus died for the church. Like the nation of Israel, the church is the people of God. It's worth fighting for. The church is worthy of our service. It's worth defending and praying for. The church is worth my time, energy, leadership, tithe, and even my life.

Like Israel, the church is under Satan's constant attack. Yet, many Christians are like Saul's army, watching the threat and hoping someone will do something, but not wanting to get too personally involved.

David didn't just say, "I love the Lord so much. I love him with all my heart." He was ready to put his life on the line. Do you ever get weary of Christians who spend a lot of time talking about how much they love Jesus, but can't be counted on to serve? They're offended if you mention tithing and can't ever seem to make it to prayer meeting.

Have you ever met a Christian with the attitude, "Hey, don't ask me to serve or give or sacrifice to the cause of Jesus. The church should be glad I showed up Sunday morning." Well, I'll bet the church is glad you showed up Sunday morning. All of Saul's army showed up; the problem is that none of them were fully committed.

The church should be glad I showed up

It might seem outrageous to suggest they weren't really committed. After all, these men went to war for their country. But they didn't have the spiritual dedication necessary to trust God when a big problem came and step out on faith. One of the best gifts a believer can give their church is the gift of personal faith. This means stepping up when the odds seem difficult and trusting the Lord to come through. For you, that might mean teaching a class when you feel it just can't be done, serving in a ministry you don't think you have time for, tithing when you already feel strapped for cash, or starting a new ministry when you're not so sure you've got what it takes.

Where's Saul?

Shouldn't Saul be taking care of this giant problem? I mean, he is the king of Israel, the leader of the nation. Not only that, the guy is huge. He doesn't even make a battle plan. He showed up to the battlefront dressed in some pretty impressive armor, but he never seems to have gotten it dirty.

I enjoyed an October 2013 Forbes.com article titled **"Excuses for Calling in Sick."** One of my favorites read,

> "Employee's false teeth flew out the window while driving down the highway."

Now I think that's actually a pretty good excuse. If your teeth fly out the window while driving, you've got to pull over and get them. Another was,

> "Employee's favorite football team lost on Sunday so needed Monday to recover."

I think I know that guy. Or,

> "Employee said that someone glued her doors and windows shut so she couldn't leave the house to come to work."

I think that person must know my kids. They love glue! How about this excuse:

> "Employee's fake eye was falling out of its socket."

Once again, that seems like a pretty good excuse to me. If your eye can't stay in the hole in your head, there's probably a problem.

So what was Saul's excuse? This is his job! He must have felt at least a little awkward when a kid stepped forward and offered to do what was rightfully his duty.

Saul was glad to pay someone else to have faith for him. He was ready to write a check, give away his daughter in marriage, and even exempt the family from taxes. In church, we can be too anxious to pay someone to do what we're supposed to do. I see people who would make great youth leaders, yet they hope the church will employ a minister of youth. People who would make wonderful directors of programs, but they hope the church will hire more staff to fill the leadership void. Thankfully, I've seen the opposite as well! I've seen godly people step up and pour their leadership abilities into the kingdom of God. I've seen God's people generously give to the Lord their skills and tithes and gifts, and when they do, giants fall.

I wonder if Saul dressed David in his armor for less honorable reasons than might first appear. Is he concerned about David? I think so. But anyone's armor would do, right? Why does the king himself give David his armor? Is it to be a means of encouragement for the boy? I don't think so. Was Saul's armor better than the other men's? That is possible. The battle is going to take place down in the valley. This is before the age of mega screens, so the details will be hard to discern for the two armies watching. Could Saul be secretly hoping his army thinks it's Saul down there fighting the battle? That might sound ridiculous, but remember, Saul was crazy.

No Observers

A friend of mine is a Marine officer. A few years ago he made a trip to Israel to observe their army as they prepared for combat. He was surprised when he checked in and they issued him a rifle and armor. He handed the rifle back and explained that he was not there to actually fire a weapon, he was just present as an observer. "There are no observers," was the quick response as the weapons were pressed back into his hand.

That is also true in God's army: there are no observers. We don't get to just show up for Bible study and fellowship—we have to be ready to serve and fight the devil on whatever battlefront he sticks his head up on.

Why God Allows Giants in Our Path

Goliath was not a surprise to God. In fact, he had ordained that crisis in the life of Israel to bring forth godly people ready to confront big issues.

The Philistines had been seafaring people. They had come from an island to the Middle East. Once they landed, they established five cities, each led by a ruthless king. The Philistines entered the Iron Age before the Israelites did, and their weapons of war were far superior. The Philistines would put swords on their chariot wheels. This allowed them to ride onto a battlefield and mow people down like grass.

Now, to make it all worse, out comes a giant Philistine over nine feet tall. Why didn't God just zap Goliath? Remove him from the world of the breathing? I think there are several reasons God forces us to face giants.

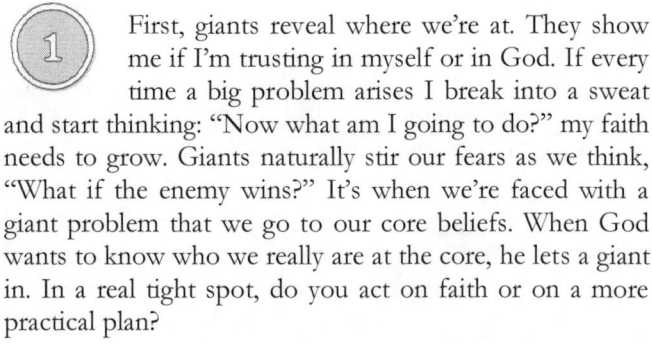 First, giants reveal where we're at. They show me if I'm trusting in myself or in God. If every time a big problem arises I break into a sweat and start thinking: "Now what am I going to do?" my faith needs to grow. Giants naturally stir our fears as we think, "What if the enemy wins?" It's when we're faced with a giant problem that we go to our core beliefs. When God wants to know who we really are at the core, he lets a giant in. In a real tight spot, do you act on faith or on a more practical plan?

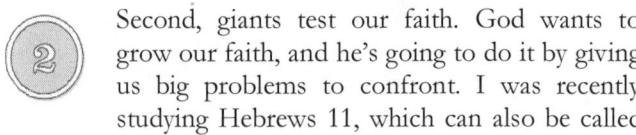 Second, giants test our faith. God wants to grow our faith, and he's going to do it by giving us big problems to confront. I was recently studying Hebrews 11, which can also be called God's Hall of Fame. It is a massive list of godly people who walked by faith. But I noticed that as the writer of Hebrews came to the end of the Old Testament, he seamlessly moved into the present age and counted people in his own generation in the Hall of Faith. The author of

Hebrews knew that the story isn't over. God is done writing the Bible, but He is not done writing the story of faith. We're part of that story. But faith doesn't get room to exercise itself unless there are giants to confront.

Third, giants open the door for miracles. If there were never any problems, we would never see God do big things. Often we want to play it so safe that we don't allow the opportunity for God to do miracles. We don't see the sea part because we feel safer as slaves in Egypt. We don't see the giant fall because it is safer to make a deal and send him away.

So what is this biblical account about? It's about serving God and giving the highest honor to God's work on Earth.

CHAPTER 3
WHEN YOU WORK FOR A JERK

How do you survive when you have to submit to someone who is less than godly? People who are arrogant, demeaning, difficult, and give you outrageous assignments?

King Saul was a very difficult boss. He manipulated situations and gave outrageous assignments—he once told David that to marry his daughter he would have to bring back a hundred Philistine foreskins. Now that's a pretty obscene assignment!

A Marine friend told me that he once worked for a boss who was absolutely sadistic. He kept a tank of piranhas in his office. He would call troops in and have them stand at attention as he chewed them out, while at the same time feeding pinky mice to the piranhas.

I think an honest assessment of the story of David and Goliath needs to also take into account the opposition David received from his own team. David's own family had some less than flattering things to say about him. Worse, King Saul was on the verge of wrecking the entire nation. He was not operating with faith, but cowardly seeking a way out of the mess. He was looking for someone to pin the blame on.

Saul was a spiritual fraud. He disobeyed God multiple times, evoking the rage of the prophet Samuel. Saul was such a bad king that he caused Samuel to mourn.

I'm curious how a young man like David survived the emotional assault Satan barraged him with. I think God gave David a healthy dose of self-perception. David did not need the affirmation of others to build himself up; he was confident in who God said he was.

The Importance of A Healthy Self-Perception

Do you like being around prideful, arrogant people? Probably not. But I'm willing to bet you also don't like hanging around people who are always putting themselves down. Some people are hard on themselves hoping others will jump in and say nice things about them. Their self-ridicule is really a way of attempting to get others to compliment them.

David's confidence was in God's assessment of him. He might come across as arrogant at first, but when we look closer I think what could be mistaken as pride is really a strong faith. He offers to

> *David's confidence was in God's assessment of him.*

fight the giant not based on his personal skills at giant killing, but based on the faithfulness of God. Because the Lord has shown him kindness in the past he is able to trust in the Lord in the giant crisis at hand.

Lie #1: You're not worthy.

Anytime you want to serve the Lord, someone will be nearby to tell you why you can't. If there isn't anyone filling that role, your own mind will offer many suggestions as to why you are not fit to serve God.

Notice some of the people who didn't feel David was up to the task:

David's brothers were probably glad to see him at first. He showed up with bread and corn and probably some kind words from their father. I'll bet he was a welcome sight. But as soon as he started asking what the king would give the person who killed Goliath, his brothers' ire was raised. Eliab in particular is said to have become angry with him. Eliab questioned David's motives, asking, "What are you really doing here, David?" He degraded David's job, asking who he had left those few sheep with. Eliab cut to David's heart, bluntly telling his brother that he was "conceited" and that his heart was "wicked." Finally, Eliab suggested that David was only interested in the show so he could go around bragging that he had been at war.

I'll bet Elliab's words hurt more than anything Goliath said to David. This was his big brother. At the heart of it, David's brother was telling him that he was not worthy to serve God on the battlefront. Eliab told him that he had no experience, he wasn't qualified, his heart was wicked, and he was full of pride. Wow, talk about sticks and stones breaking bones! This had to cut David deeply.

Satan's favorite line even today is, "You're not worthy." You want to serve God in a new ministry, but Satan will bring up your old sins and hurts. You want to have a godly walk like others, but Satan will tell you that you can't because you struggle with sin. You are hoping for a promotion at work, but the enemy reminds you of all the mistakes you've made and you feel so unqualified.

Lie #2: You're too young.

In 1 Samuel 17:33, Saul explains to David that he can't fight the Philistine because he's only a youth, and Goliath is a grown man who's been fighting since he was young.

Of course, Saul isn't a youth, but he's also not rushing out to the battlefield, is he?

I can't think of a good way to get experience at giant killing other than by taking on a giant. It's not like they had "giant simulators" where you could go and try various techniques. David is too young and too inexperienced, but Saul can't find anyone with "giant killing" on their resume.

Lie #3: The enemy is stronger.

When David comes out for battle, Goliath can't believe it. He despised him. Goliath was absolutely convinced he could defeat David because he believed he was stronger. And in terms of raw strength, Goliath was stronger.

One of Satan's tactics today is to make us feel weak and vulnerable.

Stirring Doubt

Goliath openly shared with David what he planned to do with the kid once he got his hands on him. He hoped to feed David's dead carcass to wild animals and hungry birds. Not exactly a pep talk. Satan is hoping David will start thinking, "Wait a minute, no one has ever killed a giant like this before. I don't even have a sword. I'm just a kid. What if this doesn't work? What if God doesn't come through? What if miss?" Satan plays that game with us all the time. It's called the "What If" game.

What if I continue to love my spouse, but things never change? What if I stand up for what is right, and get totally defeated? What if my reputation suffers as a result of speaking the truth? What if I reach out and try to show love in a broken relationship, only to get rejected one more time?

Stirring doubt is what the enemy is an expert in. He can't actually beat God, but he can do great damage if he convinces us that the Lord isn't really that reliable.

In the parable of the sower, Jesus described a farmer who scattered seed. Some fell on the road, where it was trampled and birds ate it. This hard path represents a hard heart.

A second handful of seed landed on rocks. The plants came up, but quickly died for lack of water. Jesus later explained that the seed that fell on rock are people who accept the Gospel with joy at first, but then fall away because of the trials of this world. Satan gets them and destroys them.

Another handful of seed fell into thorns. Naturally the thorns choked the plants. Jesus said that seed represented people who hear, but they get distracted. Things like worry and the pursuit of wealth and pleasure cause some people to never mature in the Lord. They live in a constant "What If." Doubt consumes their life and they are unable to stand against the giants. What if I don't make enough money? What if the roof caves in? What if I don't get promoted? I better work a bit longer. The result of all the what-iffing is that they fail to ever fully trust God.

For forty days, Goliath challenged the people of Israel and Judah, but they were afraid to confront him. What if he won? What if God didn't come through? What if they died? Better to play it safe, they decided. Because of their fear, they were naturalized for forty days. That's forty days they could have been home with their wives and families enjoying the land God had given them. Fear robs

Luke 8:5-8

A sower went out to sow his seed: and as he sowed, some fell by the way side; and it was trodden down, and the fowls of the air devoured it.

And some fell upon a rock; and as soon as it was sprung up, it withered away, because it lacked moisture.

And some fell among thorns; and the thorns sprang up with it, and choked it.

And other fell on good ground, and sprang up, and bare fruit an hundredfold.

us of time and the good things God has for us.

David was the final kind of seed that Jesus described. In Luke 8:15, Jesus said sometimes the word of God falls on rich soil that not only hears God's word, but retains it and produces a crop. Satan couldn't pull David down with fear or worries about this world. He stood firm in his faith and the result was a glorious harvest for the people of God.

David's Response

How did David respond to the many discouraging roadblocks Satan put in his way? Let's look at how David reacted to the three groups that sought to pull David down:

When David's brother Eliab accused him of being conceited, David simply chose to ignore him. His brother might scorn him and accuse him of being unworthy, but David didn't seem to give him any emotional ground. It was not up to Eliab to decide if David was worthy or not—God had already decided. In fact, God had anointed David king of Israel in the previous chapter. David, the anointed king, decides to behave as a child of God in the role God had already given him.

I love commentaries over movies; they give the film an extra layer of depth. However, I'm not always such a fan of commentary over life—people who have something to say about everyone else. Sometimes the best thing you can do is ignore people's commentaries on your life. You don't have to respond to every letter, email, or Facebook post. David asked his brother two questions: "Now what have I done?" suggesting they had run-ins before. Then he asked, "Can't I even say anything?" He was unwilling to let his older brother bully him emotionally. He doesn't sulk off to Jesse and tattle on Eliab; he just moves on.

Jesus said that sometimes you just have to shake the dust off your feet and move on. When words hurt, often

27

what we need to do is resist the urge to retaliate and just shake it off. David understood that his brother was not the real enemy, Goliath was. He didn't try to prove himself to his brother; he gave a simple response and moved on.

It seems that many times right before a spiritual battle, Satan tries to stir up family conflict. These wounds hurt more and the damage lasts longer. But David didn't take the devil's bait; he just hit delete on Eliab's email.

Saul suggested that David was not ready for the task at hand. Instead of caving in to the king's assessment of the youth, David set an example of what a godly king should be. Saul wasn't exactly a motivational boss. He didn't encourage young David or praise his courage and faith. But that didn't drag David down at all. In 1 Timothy 4:12, the Apostle Paul instructs young Timothy not to let anyone look down on him because of his youth, but instead he commands Timothy be the one to set an example for those around him. That's exactly what David would do for his own boss.

David, the secretly crowned king, shows king Saul what a leader is supposed to do. He sets aside the armor of war, resisting the urge to even arm himself with a warriors' sword, and instead chooses to dress like a shepherd. Saul might wear a royal robe and have great armor, but he didn't know what it meant to walk by faith as the king of Israel. In stark contrast, David chose to walk in the shadow of his forefathers as a simple shepherd. Abraham, Isaac and Jacob, and Moses had all been shepherds and God had done great things through them.

David doesn't feel the need to be something he's not. A giant needed to be knocked down, but that didn't mean that David had to pretend to be a warrior when he wasn't.

The young man showed big King Saul what the king of Israel was really supposed to be: The king of Israel was supposed to trust God to take care of the problem. The king of Israel should be the first to the battlefront, ready to face any enemy that came their way. That's how Moses had led the people. He didn't hide in a tent, but boldly stood before Pharaoh and declared, "Let my people go!" The king of Israel was to be a man who honored the Scriptures. In fact, Deuteronomy 17:18 commanded that the king personally write his own copy of the Torah and keep it near him. There's no sign Saul had done anything of the kind. If he had, he might have been inclined to behave more like a Moses and less like, well, a Saul.

Most important, the king of Israel was to see himself as a servant of God. The true king of Israel was not a monarch on an Earthly throne, but the Mighty God of Heaven. The king was just to be his Earthly agent. Saul saw himself as royalty, but David approached the situation with a servant's heart.

David put all his confidence in the Lord. God had saved him in the past, and he trusted that God wasn't going to change his mind now.

Finally, when Goliath cursed David and tried to intimidate him, David was up for the challenge. He knew which fight was worthy of his energy, and Goliath got the full measure of David's righteous anger. David did not let any of these people define or discourage him. He chose to see himself the way God saw him. God has told him that someday he would be king. He did not come away from that experience demanding people serve him, but instead seems to have all the more desire to live up to what a godly king is supposed to be. David was not concerned with title or position; knowing who he was in God's sight was enough to give him the courage he needed to do what is right.

We are the priests and kings of the new Earth. That's not a hopeful pep-talk, but the promise of Scripture. Revelation 5:10 says we are a kingdom of priests who serve God and will reign on the new Earth. Just because David had not yet been crowned king did not mean he wasn't king. God had already anointed him. If you are a follower of Jesus, God has already chosen you to reign upon the new Earth. We should live with that joyful confidence. More than simply being joyful, it is good for us to show the world how a child of God behaves.

Why Self-Perception Matters

How I see myself in Christ determines how I respond to problems the enemy will throw at me. A person with a low self-esteem never sees themselves as ready to do anything for God. They might feel a nudge to serve the Lord, but as soon as someone says maybe they're not ready, they lower their head and say, "Yeah, you're right."

Many people don't have a problem seeing themselves as too small; they have a struggle with arrogance. They demand things be done their way. A godly self-perception is in no way arrogant. In fact, a prideful spirit declares war on God. Goliath was prideful. In his pride, he felt he alone was the answer to the Philistine's problem.

How you act when the battle is over reveals the state of your heart.

David's brother accused him of pride, but that's sure not what I see in David. Notice how after the battle he never mentions Goliath again. I know I would be tempted to drop that into some conversations. David wrote many of the Psalms, but there's not a "David Killed Goliath" Psalm. I think I might have slipped it in to other Psalms: "The Lord is my shepherd, he helped me kill Goliath." But David never brags or allows his heart to get conceited.

How you act when the battle is over reveals the state of

your heart. It appears David never even asked the king for the reward that had been promised to the victor. He understood that the battle belonged to Yahweh. He was content being God's vessel.

God's Glory

I think it's interesting that the Bible says that Goliath "despised" David. I suspect the very reason God chose David is because it would stir up such condemnation from the enemy. The NIV translates 1 Corinthians 1:28-29 saying that God "chose the lowly things of this world and the despised things—and the things that are not—to nullify the things that are, so that no one may boast before Him."

When God uses weak people to do great things, boasting is out of the question. No one can say, "Look how cool I am!" because really it was God at work all along. Goliath mistook David's humility and outward appearances as weakness.

God uses humble people to do great things so that God will get the glory. Now suppose instead of sending little David out, God had raised up a great big Hebrew giant. Let's make him a foot taller than Goliath. A ten-foot giant! Impressive, right? And when Goliath came out and challenged Israel, King Saul sent his giant a text message:

> God uses humble people to do great things so that God will get the glory.

"Come on out, big boy!" What good would it have done if the Hebrew giant had beat the Philistine giant? Everyone would say, "Wow, what a great giant Israel has."

David says that because God is going to use him, all the world will know that there is a God in Israel. That is, when small David rises up against Goliath, no one can say it is because of David's might or power or strength that he took the giant down. They don't say, "Look how great

David is"; they say, "What a great God David serves."

When You Work for A Jerk

Notice four times David calls himself Saul's "servant." Only people with a godly self-esteem can handle submission. Even though Samuel had told him one day he would be king, David did not bubble with pride. Instead, he submitted to the king God had already given the nation.

Maybe you can't stand your boss. In fact, maybe you work for a jerk! Saul was a jerk, wasn't he? David was able to work for a jerk because he understood that really he was God's servant, not Saul's. Maybe you're thinking, "But my boss is a lot worse than King Saul." Well, according to the Bible, King Saul was demon-possessed. That could make him a bit tough to work for.

If you have a difficult boss, I encourage you to make a personal commitment to honor authority even though it is difficult. God made Saul King, and David chose to honor that. Romans 13:1 tells us that everyone must obey those over us because they are there as a result of the Lord's own hand. No one has slipped into power outside of God's will.

The Apostle Paul asked us in Colossians 3:23 to do everything as if we were working for the Lord, not men. That was David's secret, wasn't it? He didn't really see himself working for Saul so much as he understood he was a servant of God. It is difficult for me to go in a store and listen to employees complain about management or the hours they've been given or their petty gripes about other employees. That kind of attitude won't get those people far because it is dishonoring the authority God has put over them.

Parents, if you want successful children, it's not just about good grades and college, though both those things are great. Make your children respect you—I'm not saying abuse them. It is your job to teach them to honor those in authority. Our culture hates authority, but a young person who can honor those above them will go far in life.

You can only submit with that kind of self-confidence when your self-worth is not defined by the world but by God. When you understand that Christ laid down his life for you and made you his child, it is a lot easier to honor authority. More than that, we are actually able to love those above us because we realize that somehow the God we love is working through them and has put them there for his purposes. But submission is not for the weak of heart.

Healthy People Inspire Others

Did you notice how many people it took to defeat the Philistines? David started it out by defeating Goliath; but the rest of the Philistines were slaughtered by the men of Israel and Judah. 1 Samuel 17:53 tells us that the Israelites plowed into the Philistines, waging brutal warfare on them. In fact, they chased the Philistines all the way to Goliath's hometown of Gath, as well as the city of Ekron. This was not a one-man war, this was a team effort. God used one man with faith to rally the faith of others.

We all need a David in our life to rally us to our best. Beloved, you're not good enough to stand alone—no one is. That's why God gave you the Holy Spirit and the church. Neither of these were our idea. No one said, "Now God, I can't handle these problems in life on my own, send me the Holy Spirit. And while you're at it, connect me deeply with a church family." No, it was at God's initiation that he gave us his presence in the form of the Holy Spirit and the companionship of others.

Would you like a healthier work environment? Here's what I notice: Healthy people tend to inspire others to behave better. If you choose to respect your boss instead of gossiping, others will soon begin to notice. That's real leadership. Showing respect to broken people, love to leaders who do not have their game together, requires people who know exactly who they are in Christ Jesus.

CHAPTER 4
A GOOD OLD FASHIONED
BIBLICAL STONING

One of the easily overlooked elements of this story is the importance of the name of God.

Goliath cursed David by his gods. In fact, Goliath seems have been cursing Israel from the beginning of the story. But did he go further? Did he not only curse David and the nation of Israel, did he curse God? The text doesn't say so directly, but David seems to think he did. If in the mix of curses, Goliath called down one of those curses against the name Yahweh, then he had committed blasphemy.

Robert D. Bergen, author of the 1&2 Samuel volume of the *New American Commentary*, stresses that Goliath did indeed curse God's name. Bergen writes, "David expressed awareness that Goliath had committed a capital crime by insulting, and thus blaspheming, the God of Israel" (p. 195).

Many times in Scripture, God revealed to mankind the seriousness of blasphemy. The third commandment is that no one should misuse the name. But that's not all! The

Hebrews were also not to let anyone who does blaspheme the name get away with it. That's part of the commandment: they must protect God's name.

In Leviticus 24:16 God reveals exactly what is to happen to a person who blasphemes: "Anyone who blasphemes the name of the LORD must be put to death. The entire assembly must stone him. Whether an alien or native-born, when he blasphemes the Name, he must be put to death" (NIV).

Now notice that this is a "whoever" command. Even the pagan nations must obey this. And the penalty for cursing the name of Yahweh is the same for both the foreigner and the Hebrew. If they blaspheme the name of God they "must" be put to death. It doesn't matter if they are an Israelite or an Egyptian or a Philistine; the same rules apply.

David, a Torah observant Hebrew, carried out the letter

> **Leviticus 24:16**
>
> And he that blasphemeth the name of Yahweh, he shall surely be put to death, and all the congregation shall certainly **stone him**: as well the stranger
>
> (KJV)

of the law precisely. The punishment for blasphemy was stoning—so David stoned him. He then finished the job with Goliath's own blade.

Honoring God's Name

God is serious about how we treat his name.

Few people get to name themselves. My wife and I carefully chose each of our four daughter's names. We wanted to name our second daughter Annie, but were concerned that it might not be a proper enough name. "What if she gets nominated to the Supreme Court?" I mused. So, we named her Anna, but call her Annie. Of course, she won't answer to the name Anna.

Names are important. To give someone or something a name is an expression of dominion. Adam showed dominion when he named the animals. Have you ever wondered who named God? Well, no one did. God named Himself! His name, Yahweh, means "I AM."

A literal translation of Exodus 20:7 warns us, "You shall not lift up the name of Yahweh your God for nothingness."

One way we dishonor God's name is by cursing. I think this is what Goliath did. In his sermon, *God's Hall Of Fame*, Dr. Adrian Rogers talked about his friend, Paul Anderson. Rogers said that Anderson was once titled "The Strongest Man in the World." Guinness deemed his lifting of 6,270 pounds as the greatest weight ever lifted by a human being.

Paul Anderson

One day, according to Dr. Rogers, Anderson was going through an airport when he heard someone curse and then say, "Jesus Christ!" Paul ran to the man and picked him up. Can you imagine that person's surprise? They were suddenly lifted into the air by the strongest man in the world!

"Did you say Jesus Christ?" Anderson asked. "Where is he? Show me! I want to see him!"

Looking down in disbelief at Paul Anderson, the man said, "Oh my God!"

Anderson dropped the man, declaring, "That's him!"

Other ways we abuse God's name is treating it like magic or using God's name impulsively. I'm really startled by the abuse of the letters O-M-G. There are certain channels on TV that I will not watch because they so frequently show people declaring God's name inappropriately. We abuse God's name by treating it like magic. God's name is not a secret trick to beat the devil. Speaking His name does not give us powers. In fact, in Acts 19 we find a Jew who had only heard about the power of Jesus and how Paul drove out demons in Jesus' name. His seven sons tried to drive out an evil spirit in Jesus' name. The man with the evil spirit said, "I know who Jesus is, and I know who Paul is, but I sure don't know who you are!" And that demon-possessed man gave them such a beating they ran from the house naked and bleeding. The devil wasn't afraid of a magic trick then and he's not now. What Satan fears are people who actually know God!

Another way we abuse God's name is by using it as an excuse. Such as when a person ends a relationship by saying, "I've been praying, and I think God wants me to break up with you." When the truth is, very little prayer was put into the subject—God is simply introduced to spiritualize the decision. God doesn't want us to use Him as a cover for ourselves.

I think televangelists abuse God's name when they use it to manipulate others. When someone says, "The Lord told me if we don't get a thousand dollars, we'll go off the air," they are dishonoring the Commandment. We should never try and get money from someone using the name of Jesus.

Think I'm over-reacting? Ask young David as he loads up his slingshot to carry out God's command. No joke, God is very serious about how we treat his name.

David Knew God

David did not beat Goliath simply because he knew a magic formula that, when spoken, would knock down a giant. David knew the God behind the name.

Psalm 9:10 declares that those who know God's name will trust in Him because Yahweh has not forgotten those who seek him. To know God is to know his character. Proverbs 18:10 tells us that the name of Yahweh is a strong tower, it is a place of safety where the righteous can take refuge. David, a righteous young man, did just that: he took refuge in the name of Yahweh.

David boldly told Goliath, "I come against you in the name of Yahweh of Hosts." That is like saying, "All you see is me, Goliath, but really there is a spiritual army amassed all around me. Heaven's armies have gathered for war, and God is their commander. The God who leads the warriors of Heaven is going to give me victory."

How did David see what Goliath did not? He saw with spiritual eyes, not just physical. He saw with faith while Goliath saw simply with sight. We should know anytime we have to deal with the enemy, the commander of the Lord's army is near us.

A friend of mine said, "I hate when I'm about to hang up from leaving a voicemail and say, 'In Jesus' name, Amen.'" By declaring God's Holy Name, David tells Goliath, "This voicemail is over. I'm done messing with you."

Run!

Goliath asked David to come close so they could have what the seasoned warrior considered a fair fight. Usually someone with a slingshot would keep their distance, but David did just what Goliath requested of him. He ran toward the giant and fired his slingshot. David deliberately chose not to put on Saul's armor. If he had, it would have been like two big tanks lugging toward each other. Actually, David would not have been like a tank at all! But without the armor, David is quick on his feet and is able to charge the giant.

Malcolm Gladwell has written a delightful book about David and Goliath titled *David and Goliath: Underdogs, Misfits, and the Art of Battling Giants*. He offers some great insights into just how powerful a skilled man with a slingshot could have been. At the heart of it, Gladwell suggests that David brought a gun to a sword fight. He chose not to arm up like Goliath and play by the Philistines' rules of war.

As he surveyed little David, I wonder if Goliath had a moment of realization—he was over-dressed for the occasion. In fact, with a boy running at him (Goliath had called him forward!) and the stone suddenly in the air, Goliath did not have any maneuverability. He was a huge sitting duck.

It's amazing how the devil miscalculated this one, isn't it? Imagine spiritually, as that rock shoots through the air, there is a moment when the angels are going nuts. That must have been an incredible split second—to watch that slingshot snap forward and the stone swim through the air, then finally chew into its target. The great cloud of witnesses described in Hebrews 13 must have been like a stadium, roaring with delight that day as the rock struck the giant and he went down like a massive tree. I imagine it felt like an earthquake.

> **It's amazing how the devil miscalculated this one!**

In Numbers 13:27, the original spies who looked over Canaan were concerned that they could not take Canaan because there were giants in the land. The account of David and Goliath gives us a hint of what might have happened if the people had acted in faith and had taken on those giants instead of heading back into the wilderness for another forty-year hike.

Dog Gone Dagon

Goliath cursed David by his gods. He would have been a worshiper of the Philistine god, Dagon. He should have thought twice before invoking his gods' names.

Yahweh seems to take particular pleasure in messing with Dagon. I believe that behind many false idols are demons that appear to give them power. In 1 Corinthians 10:20, Paul gave us the insight that pagans, like Goliath, offer their sacrifices to demons. No wonder false gods can appear to have power and magic, the dark force of the enemy lies behind them.

There's really no reason to feel sorry for a demon, but whatever fallen angel had the assignment of inhabiting Dagon really got a raw deal. In 1 Samuel 5, the Philistines managed to capture the of Ark of the Covenant. They thought it was their greatest victory against their old foe, Israel. In fact, the Philistines were so proud of their plunder that they marched the Ark into the temple of Dagon.

The Ark is the Earthly throne of the living God. It was carried in front of the people when Israel moved through the wilderness to show God's kingship over the nation. When Israel was not on the move, the Ark was placed behind the curtain in the Holy of Holies. The top of the Ark was the mercy seat crowned by two cherubim with wings that arched over it. The mercy seat was the symbol of God's throne, and He sat enthroned between the cherubim (see 1 Samuel 4:4). God's physical presence among the people was represented in the Ark of the Covenant.

Imagine an idol that is the home of a demon. Then think the Ark of the Covenant, which is the throne of God, is carried into that demon's temple. Think the demon was a bit nervous? Oh, you bet!

The temple of Dagon was in the city of Ashdod. When the people got up the next morning, they must have been so excited to rush to their temple and glory in Dagon's victory. But when they arrived, they discovered something terrible had happened: Dagon had fallen on his face in front of the Ark. Now that's embarrassing! Of course, they took the time to put Dagon back in his place, but no celebration is recorded. It's a little difficult to gloat when your idol falls on its face in front of the Ark of Yahweh.

So what happened that night to cause Dagon to fall on his face? This is just how I imagine it; it's not in the Bible.

Think of the demon assigned to that idol, shivering as the Ark of God sits before him. From his Earthly throne in the dark of that temple, God might have said, "Dagon, bow."

"No!" the demon might have shrieked. But he had no choice; he was going down. Just as on that final day every knee shall bow and every tongue confess the name of Jesus, the demon inside Dagon was forced to bow down before the throne of God.

The destruction of Dagon by Philip James de Loutherbourg, 1793

When the people came and put him upright, I wonder if that demon was sweating bullets by then. "Don't leave me in here with that thing!" he might have been crying.

Foolishly, the Philistines left their god alone one more night with the living God. When they arrived the next day, Dagon had been completely humiliated. Not only had he fallen face first in front of the Ark, but his head and hands had broken off. God decapitated him! I just wonder what happened that night between the demon and Yahweh. The Bible doesn't record the battle, just the results. The idol's head had landed at the threshold of the temple. How did his head get thrown all the away across that huge temple and land in the doorway? It is the sign of a devastating fight in which Dagon lost big time. Whatever happened that night between Yahweh and that demon sure wasn't pretty. The further loss of Dagon's hands was a way of revealing that he was powerless before God.

The populace of Ashdod seems to have been a little

41

slow to understand what was happening. They had declared war on the One True God. Soon, not only was their god broken and humiliated in his own temple, but the people began to break out with tumors.

The Philistines decided it was time to move the Ark. Imagine the mayor at the city council meeting shouting, "Get that thing out of here!"

Where did they move it? To Gath—Goliath's hometown! Once again, as at Ashdod, the people broke out in tumors.

Goliath must have been aware of Dagon's humiliating defeat against Yahweh. His people finally got so scared of Yahweh that they sent the Ark back loaded with gifts. But Goliath brazenly cursed David by his gods. So Yahweh allowed Goliath to go down the same way his god went down.

Goliath fell face first, the same way Dagon had fallen before the Ark. Falling on his face in front of David, it is as if the giant is actually bowing before God who towered invisibly over young the boy. If Goliath wanted to invoke Dagon's name, then he could die like Dagon. David quickly ran up to the giant and cut off his head. Interesting, since in the battle at Dagon's temple, God himself had decapitated Dagon.

Don't Be Intimidated

We're surrounded. The devil has his bullhorn and is yelling at the people of God: "You are surrounded! Put your hands in the air and surrender. Step back slowly into the world and re-assimilate yourselves."

Satan persistently finds sneaky ways to try and get us to give up on the church and Godly living. Sometimes the devil just pulls out all stops and goes crazy on you. Have you ever had a week where the devil just threw everything he had on you? He dropped a giant on Israel!

When we're faced with giants, what are we tempted to do? Some are tempted to pass the buck, let someone else handle the problem—that's what Saul wanted to do. Some are tempted to run and hide. Some are tempted to surrender to the enemy. Why put up a fight when the world is so attractive? But there are some who resist these temptations and rise up against the enemy. Even though the problem looks impossible, they move by faith and it is then that we see the moving of God.

David tells Goliath, it's not me who is surrounded—it's you! You are surrounded by the unseen armies of the heavenly hosts.

CHAPTER 5
THE FUTURE LOOKS GREAT

What David did to Goliath didn't just win a temporary battle, but set the stage for the rest of David's life.

Who Killed Goliath?

Not only was the army of Israel inspired that day to wage a ruthless war against the Philistines, I think David's own mighty men took personal comfort in what happened to their leader. David's courage called out greatness in them.

There is an interesting story recounted in 1 Chronicles 20:5 in which we are told that one of David's mighty men, Elhanan, killed a giant named Lahmi, who was none less than Goliath's brother. However, 2 Samuel 21:19 actually says that Elhanan killed Goliath himself. Wait a minute! What's going on here? Did Elhanan kill Goliath's brother, or Goliath? And if he killed Goliath, who did David kill?

Some suggest that David did not kill Goliath at all, but that it was Elhanan all along. They think that since Elhanan was unknown, the hero of the story was changed to the more popular David in the account in 1 Samuel. Such a view dismisses the inspiration of Scripture and is a direct affront on the integrity of the biblical writers.

If you're a *Star Wars* fan, track with me for a moment. What if I told you that Luke Skywalker blew up the Death Star? That's true, right? But what if I said to you that the Death Star was destroyed by Lando Calrissian? That's true, too, if you saw *Return of the Jedi*. What you have to know is that there were two Death Stars, thus two battles and two victors. "Death Star" was a title for a battle station, just as Goliath was a title for a warrior. There is also a sense that all Philistines are "brothers." So indicating that Elhanan killed the "brother" of Goliath is to say that he killed a Philistine who bore the title Goliath but was actually named Lahmi.

Why does the Bible tell us twice that Elhanan killed a Goliath? It's significant because he was one of David's elite warriors. How many times had he heard the story of his leader, David, taking down the original Goliath? Such tales certainly boosted his courage and faith, and may have even stirred some of his competitive nature. It wasn't David who killed Goliath, or Elhanan, but in both accounts it was God—the same God who killed Goliath killed other warriors in the days to come.

the same God who killed Goliath killed other warriors in the days to come.

God doesn't change. That is what David explained to Saul, isn't it? The same God who rescued him from lions and bears would rescue him from the Philistine. And the same God who delivered David from Goliath would later give Elhanan victory over his Goliath. And if God would help David against a lion and a bear, then again help David against a giant, and later help Elhanan against his Golaith—don't you think he will help you with your future

Goliaths?

Have you ever killed a giant only to learn he's got a brother? There are more Goliaths out there, but thankfully, the same God who gave your victory in the past will take care of you tomorrow.

Goliath's Sword

David killed Goliath by taking the giant's sword from him and driving it into him. Then he cut off Goliath's head. Before the age of the guillotine, removing a head was not an easy thing to do. However, with such a huge sword, the young man does not appear to have had any problem taking care of business right there on the battlefield.

Goliath's sword appears a second time in Scripture.

After David married King Saul's daughter, Michal, King Saul went crazy and decided to kill his son-in-law. Saul sent men to take David into custody, but Michal helped David escape out the window and stuffed the bed with goat's hair. She told the men that David was ill. David ran for his life and went to Nob, where he found an order of priests who were busy serving God.

The priest at Nob gave the hungry David bread from the table. David ate the consecrated bread, promising the priest that his men had been behaving in a manner that honored God. David asked for one more thing: a weapon. David asked the priest if he had a sword or a spear with which he hoped might defend himself against angry King Saul and his men if he had to. The priest did indeed have a weapon for David, and it was no ordinary thing: he had Goliath's sword wrapped in cloth behind the ephod, the priest's robe. I think they kept the sword near the robe for two reasons: one was to hide the famous weapon, and another was to remind them of God's greatness every time they dressed for worship.

Imagine how David felt as the priest placed that familiar sword in David's hands. He must have remembered how heavy it was, and remembered that great moment that he cut off the giant's head. "There is no sword like it," David told the priest.

David fled from there to Goliath's hometown of Gath. Think he was a bit afraid? What if Goliath's own people figured out who he was and decided to exact some sweet revenge? But with Goliath's own sword at his side, he certainly didn't doubt the bigness of God. Possession of the sword was a subtle reminder that God was faithful, big and powerful—and that Goliath was dead. By the way, the priests at Nob would later pay a high price for giving David Goliath's sword: King Saul had them executed.

I wonder how long David had Goliath's sword. It's hard to imagine him parting ways with it too quickly. Did he carry it into battle against the Philistines at Keilah (1 Samuel 23:5)? David hid from Saul in caves and in the rocks of the desert. I love how Saul dipped into a cave to go to the bathroom, not knowing it was the very cave David was hiding in! All of David's men couldn't believe it. "This is our chance!" they told David. Were they eyeing David's sword? Would David slay the king of Israel with the very same sword he'd killed Golaith?

Instead of killing King Saul, David sharply rebuked his men. King Saul was not the enemy; he was the Lord's anointed. Eliab had once opposed David, who was also the Lord's anointed. David shows that unlike his big brother, he refused to even speak badly of the Lord's anointed.

David snuck up behind Saul and cut off a sliver of Saul's robe. Did he use Goliath's sword to do that? Interesting if he did. When Saul came outside, David confronted him with the cut robe in his hand. "You are not my enemy," he seems to have said to David. Imagine him touching Goliath's sword. Here is the enemy! Philistines are the enemy. But then, holding in his other hand the king's cut robe, he said, "You are my king! Don't listen to people who say I'm out to hurt you." The sword of war became a tool of peace in David's hand.

By the way, I discussed earlier that some people argue that David never killed Goliath. However, that creates quite a problem, since David took possession of Goliath's sword before Elhanan's battle with a Goliath. I guess those people believe in time warp.

Goliath's Head

Remember the joke, "David killed Goliath and cut off his head, showing that David knew how to get ahead in life."

Just as the Lord cut off Goliath's god—Dagon's head—David cut off Goliath's head. Both Dagon and Dagon's servant lost their head. But what did David do with it? After the battle, David appeared before King Saul with the giant's head still in his hand. Gross! But when you're seventeen and you kill a giant, you don't let go of that thing too quickly.

Don't you think he took that puppy home and put it in his room? Want to bother your brothers? Offer to let them kiss the giant's head goodnight before bed. I'll bet that would get under Eliab and Abinadab's skin!

Imagine David's mom talking to Jesse: "Tell David to clean his room! And that giant's head has got to go. I'm fed up with it. The thing stinks to high Heaven. It's worse than Eliabs' socks."

Well what did David really do with Goliath's head? In a simple note, half a verse, the author of Samuel tells us that David took the Philistine's head to Jerusalem (1 Samuel 17:54). But why? Jerusalem was not the capital of Israel. The city was still controlled by Jebusites who had never been driven out of the land God had given His people.

I think David did this as an act of sheer intimidation. I suspect he may have mounted Goliath's head right outside the city gate. Imagine the poor gatekeeper who opens the city for business, only to discover someone has left a giant's head on a pole outside their city.

The first city David attacked when he became the anointed king of Israel was Jerusalem (2 Sam. 5:6). In fact, in 2 Samuel 3 all the elders of the nation come and anoint David King at Hebron. Three verses later, in verse six, the thirty-year-old king attacks Jerusalem. David made the commitment to take Jerusalem when he was seventeen, and as a grown man he followed through on that decision.

When he came to Jerusalem, the Jebusites mocked him, saying that even the blind and lame among them could fight him off. David must have remembered that giant! Remember how Goliath laughed at David, telling him it just couldn't be done? You can almost hear the Jebusites ask, "Are we dogs that you come at with sticks? Even the blind among us can fight you off."

"Yeah," David might have thought, "But the same God who gave me that giant will give me this city."

Indeed, David captured the fortress at Jerusalem and named it "The City of David." He built up the city around it and under his leadership the city became a regional powerhouse. Jerusalem would become the most important city in the world, both in this world and the kingdom to come.

CONCLUSION
PASTORAL ASSURANCES

Let me give you some pastoral assurances from this story. These are things I've shared with you throughout this small book, but want to reiterate before we leave the campfire.

First, the story of David and Goliath teaches us that God's kingdom is worth our sacrifice. Life is about serving God.

Second, God does not see us the way the world sees us. Knowing that simple truth can transform our personality. Seeing ourselves with a godly perspective will make us a better family member, a better employee, and a great servant of God. The Lord can use humble people in great ways because they always return the glory to God.

Third, God is hard at work even when we do not see it. Goliath could not have seen the armies of Heaven gathered for war against him, he just saw puny Israel. But David was well aware of the spiritual nature of the battle and called on Yahweh of Hosts to come to his aid. We should be very aware that more is going on around us than we see.

Finally, there are always more battles ahead. It seems every Goliath has a brother and every problem a near cousin. Our faith should be growing, so we are always ready to take on ever bigger challenges.

When my daughter Sharon was little, our associate pastor, Grover, invited her to go up on the roof of the church with him. It was quite a daunting task! Little Sharon started up the ladder, but she was really scared. The ladder to the roof isn't at an angle; it just goes straight up, past the ceiling tiles into the attic and up to a hatch that leads to the roof. Grover talked her one rung at a time until they finally reached the roof.

"It was wonderful!" she reported on her safe return. "I could see the entire city! I could see the Marine base. You've never been up there," she said to her sisters, "but I have!"

Many times after that when she was afraid to do something big, we would say, "Now if you could climb all the way to the top of the church, certainly you can do that other thing."

Victories in our past serve to build our faith for battles in the future. The same God who knocked down Goliath is the God we serve. He is the God who also knocked down the wall at Jericho and knocked down the stone in front of Jesus' tomb. There isn't anything Satan can do to stop a servant of God from doing the work God calls us to do now and in the days to come. With God, the future looks great.

FIRELIGHT BIBLE STUDIES

JUDGES,
THE WILD WEST OF THE BIBLE

AVAILABLE AT AMAZON.COM

Made in the USA
San Bernardino, CA
29 August 2014